12 IMMIGRANTS WHO MADE
AMERICAN ARTS GREAT

by Tristan Poehlmann

www.12StoryLibrary.com

12-Story Library is an imprint of Bookstaves.

Photographs ©: Mario Ruiz/The LIFE Images Collection/Getty Images, cover, 1; F. Holland Day/PD, 4; Everett Collection Inc/Alamy Stock Photo, 6; Apic/RETIRED/Getty Images, 8; neftali/Shutterstock.com, 9; PD, 10; © Estate of Martín Ramírez, Courtesy Ricco/Maresca Gallery, 11; Oldrich/Shutterstock.com, 11; Henry Groskinsky/The LIFE Images Collection/Getty Images, 12; Macedonian Museum of Contemporary Art/CC4.0, 13; Mario Ruiz/The LIFE Images Collection/Getty Images, 14; dontworry/CC3.0, 15; Anders Krusberg/Peabody Awards/CC2.0, 16; qwesy qwesy/CC3.0, 17; Vbh massistant/CC4.0, 18; JP PULLOS/Patrick McMullan via Getty Images, 19; Greg Gibson/Associated Press, 20; David Shankbone/CC3.0, 22; John D. & Catherine T. MacArthur Foundation- used with permission, 24; BIHZAD/PD, 25; Gina Ferazzi/Los Angeles Times via Getty Images, 26; elvistudio/Shutterstock.com, 27; Everett Historical/Shutterstock.com, 28; Edward Steichen/PD, 2

ISBN
978-1-63235-572-0 (hardcover)
978-1-63235-626-0 (paperback)
978-1-63235-687-1 (ebook)

Library of Congress Control Number: 2018937976

Printed in the United States of America
Mankato, MN
June 2018

About the Cover

Video artist Nam June Paik in 1989.

Access free, up-to-date content on this topic plus a full digital version of this book. Scan the QR code on page 31 or use your school's login at 12StoryLibrary.com.

Table of Contents

Kahlil Gibran's Poetry Speaks to Millions

The poems of Kahlil Gibran are recited at weddings and funerals. Lines are quoted in speeches and songs. His book *The Prophet* has sold tens of millions of copies around the world. His wise words have inspired countless people.

Gibran was born in Lebanon in 1883. He grew up in a small clifftop village. Gibran's mother encouraged his interest in art. His father was violent and bad with money. In 1891, Gibran's father was put in jail for a crime. The family lost everything. They feared the growing religious violence in the area. In 1895, Gibran immigrated to the United States with his mother and siblings. He was 12 years old.

As a young man, Gibran studied art and literature in Boston, Massachusetts; Beirut, Lebanon; and Paris, France. In 1911, he moved to New York City. He wrote poems and stories in Arabic and English. His first book in English, *The Madman*, was published in 1918. A book of his drawings followed in 1919.

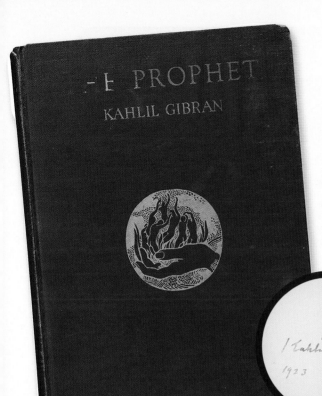

Published in 1923, *The Prophet* made him famous. In the book, a holy man named Almustafa gives advice about love, marriage, work, children, freedom, and tolerance. People could relate to the poems. They felt that Gibran was writing about their lives. *The Prophet* became an international best seller. It has never gone out of print.

THINK ABOUT IT

Gibran wrote mostly in Arabic and translated his books into English. What are some of the challenges of translating poetry from one language to another?

50
Number of languages *The Prophet* has been translated into.

- Gibran emigrated from Lebanon to the United States at age 12.
- He wrote poetry and stories in Arabic and English.
- His third book, *The Prophet*, became a worldwide best seller.

Claude McKay's Poetry Sparks an Arts Movement

The Harlem Renaissance was a golden age in black American culture. Harlem is a neighborhood in New York City. During the 1920s, many black artists and intellectuals moved there. Claude McKay played an important part in the Harlem Renaissance.

McKay was born in Jamaica in 1889. His parents raised him to be proud of their African heritage. McKay's older brother taught him English poetry. Soon McKay started to write poems. In 1912, his poetry books *Songs of Jamaica* and *Constab Ballads* were published. McKay won an award for his poetry. He used the money to immigrate to the United States for college.

In 1914, McKay moved to Harlem. He worked and wrote there for several years. In 1919, his poem "If We Must Die" was published in the magazine *Liberator.* The poem protested mob violence against black Americans. The poem was included in McKay's 1922 book *Harlem Shadows*. It has since inspired people around the world.

10

Age in years when McKay started to write poems.

- McKay emigrated from Jamaica to go to college in the United States.
- His protest poetry made him famous in the 1920s.
- His first novel, *Home to Harlem*, became a best seller.

THE JAZZ AGE

Harlem in the 1920s was full of jazz music. Born in New Orleans, jazz became the music of urban American life. Its modern energy and surprising rhythms led to new dance crazes. Jazz fever spread all the way to Paris, France and London, England.

McKay was the first major poet of the Harlem Renaissance. His protest poetry made him famous among black artists and writers. His first novel, *Home to Harlem*, was published in 1928. It was the first best-selling novel by a black writer.

IF WE MUST DIE

IF we must die—let it not be like hogs
Hunted and penned in an inglorious spot,
While round us bark the mad and hungry dogs,
Making their mock at our accursed lot.
If we must die—oh, let us nobly die,
So that our precious blood may not be shed
In vain; then even the monsters we defy
Shall be constrained to honor us though dead!

Oh, kinsmen! We must meet the common foe;
Though far outnumbered, let us still be brave,
And for their thousand blows deal one death-blow!
What though before us lies the open grave?
Like men we'll face the murderous, cowardly pack,
Pressed to the wall, dying, but—fighting back!

Mark Rothko's Paintings Change the Shape of Art

Mark Rothko was one of the greatest artists of his generation. He helped to create a new movement in American art called Abstract Expressionism. The artists believed that simple images could express complex thoughts.

Rothko was born in Russia in 1903. His family was Jewish. Violence against Jews had been growing in the area for years. When Rothko was 10 years old, his family immigrated to the United States to escape the violence. They settled in Portland, Oregon, in 1913.

In high school, Rothko won a scholarship to Yale University. He went to college for two years but did not like it. Other students treated him badly because he was an immigrant. In 1923, Rothko left college. He moved to New York City to study painting.

Rothko's artwork developed slowly. In 1929, he started teaching art to

children. He liked the simple shapes and symbols children use in art. To Rothko, they seemed like building blocks for creating complex ideas. Rothko wanted to express emotions as simple shapes. He began to make huge paintings of rectangles full of color and light. He wanted viewers to feel what he felt.

By the 1950s, Rothko's art was known around the world. One of his best-known paintings is *Orange and Yellow* from 1956.

A 2015 commemorative stamp of Rothko's *Orange and Yellow* painting.

Mark Rothko

44 USA

ABSTRACT TITLES FOR ABSTRACT PAINTINGS

Rothko didn't like to give his paintings titles. He thought titles explained too much. He wanted his paintings to speak for themselves. In the mid-1940s, he started calling paintings *Untitled* or by their colors, like *Yellow, Cherry, Orange.* Often, he just numbered them, like *No. 1* or *No. 20.*

$87 million
Amount one of Rothko's paintings sold for in 2012.

- Rothko's family emigrated from Russia to escape violence.
- He moved to New York City to study art in 1923.
- He became famous for painting symbolic shapes and colors.

Martín Ramírez's Drawings Reveal Modern Landscapes

One of America's best modern artists never saw his art in a show. Martín Ramírez created hundreds of stunning drawings. Few people heard of his work until after his death.

Ramírez was born in Mexico in 1895. His father was a farmer. Ramírez liked to draw and ride his horse. In 1918, he married, and in 1923, he bought a small ranch. To pay for the land, Ramírez needed a second job. In 1925, he immigrated to the United States. His wife and children stayed behind.

Ramírez worked in California for five years, on the railroads and in the mines. He sent money home in his letters. He drew on the letters. Then, in 1929, the Great Depression hit. Ramírez lost his job. He became homeless. In 1931, the police picked

500
Number of Ramírez's drawings known to have survived.

- Ramírez emigrated from Mexico in 1925 to find work.
- He created modern landscape art while living in a mental hospital.
- His first major show took place 10 years after his death.

THINK ABOUT IT

Ramírez never went to art school. He taught himself how to draw. What are the advantages of getting a formal education as an artist? What are the disadvantages?

him up. He was sent to a hospital for people with mental illness.

In 1948, Ramírez was sent to a state mental hospital. He lived there for the rest of his life. He passed the time by working on his art. He drew landscapes of Mexico and California. He drew horses, cowboys, trains, and churches from memory. His work was full of pattern and movement. He used lines to create depth and distance on flat paper.

Ramírez died in 1963. The first major show of his art took place in Chicago in 1973. Today he is considered an important modern artist. One of his best-known drawings is *Untitled (Horse and Rider)* from 1954.

Chryssa's Sculptures Light Up New York City

Before Chryssa, neon light was used mostly for advertising. She turned it into art. She used colorful neon tubes to create images. Today her glowing neon sculptures are found in major museums.

Chryssa was born in Greece in 1933. Her family was educated and powerful. Chryssa began painting as a teenager. Her parents sent her to Paris, France, to study art. But Chryssa wanted to go to the United States. She thought there would be more freedom to express herself. She wanted to be known by her first name only. In 1954, she immigrated to go to art school. She was 21 years old.

Chryssa moved to New York City to join the art scene. She visited

Times Square. The busy square was full of lights and advertising. The huge neon signs and the newspaper headlines inspired her. Chryssa's artwork began to include large letters and bits of text. They reminded her of secret codes. Written communication fascinated her. Chryssa began to make sculptures out of newspapers and old signs. She assembled bits and pieces to create unreadable texts.

2

Number of years Chryssa worked on her sculpture *The Gates of Times Square.*

- Chryssa emigrated from Greece in 1954 to study art.
- She was a painter and sculptor who went by her first name only.
- She became known for her innovative use of neon light in sculpture.

In the early 1960s, Chryssa began to use neon lighting in her sculptures. She was one of the first artists to experiment with neon. In 1962, she created *Times Square Sky*, her first major neon sculpture. Her most famous sculpture is *The Gates of Times Square* from 1966. Viewers walked through a set of huge blinking neon gates. Chryssa was an innovator of using technology in art.

6

Nam June Paik Invents Video Art

Nam June Paik is known as the father of video art. He was the first video artist ever, and the first artist to use a portable video camera. He turned video and TV into tools for artists.

Paik was born to a wealthy family in Korea in 1932. In 1950, they fled to escape the Korean War. Paik went to college in Japan. Then he moved to Germany to study music. In the late 1950s, Paik met a group of artists. These artists liked to experiment with new ideas. They used chance and improvisation to create their artwork. They created art in public as performances. Paik joined the group. He made music using whistles and eggbeaters. In 1963, he put on a performance using TV broadcasts.

Paik immigrated to the Unites States in 1964. In New York City, he began to focus on video. When the first portable video cameras became available in 1965, Paik bought one. He learned how to use new technology to make a new kind of art. In 1971, he created *TV Cello*. It was a working cello built from a stack of TVs. In 1974, he wrote about an "electronic superhighway," like the Internet.

HOME VIDEOS

Today you can record video on your phone. But in 1965, people recorded on cameras the size of backpacks. Video was a new technology. The ability to record daily life was new. Home videos became popular in the late 1960s. People watched their videos on their TVs.

24
Number of TVs Paik used in his 1963 artwork *TV Clock*.

- Nam June Paik emigrated from Korea with his family to escape war.
- He became known in the late 1960s for his use of technology in art.
- He is considered the father of video art.

Christo and Jeanne-Claude Wrap the World in Art

Christo and Jeanne-Claude were big thinkers. The husband-and-wife team wrapped whole buildings and islands in cloth. The environment was their canvas.

They were born on the exact same day in 1935. He was born in Bulgaria, she was born in Morocco. Both came from wealthy families. They met in Paris, France, in 1958. They fell in love and started making art together.

Christo and Jeanne-Claude wanted to create large-scale outdoor art. Their art was temporary but visually stunning. Their first artwork was *Stacked Oil Barrels* in 1961. They worked as partners and came up with ideas together. He drew and designed plans. She organized the creation of their work. In 1964, the couple moved to the United States. They were undocumented immigrants until 1967.

Living in New York City, Christo and Jeanne-Claude planned ambitious new artwork. They wanted to wrap structures in huge pieces of cloth. In the late 1960s, they wrapped a tower in Italy and a museum in Chicago. They wrapped over a mile of coastline in Sydney, Australia.

Because their art was temporary, it was often a communal event. In 2005, five million people walked through *The Gates* in New York's Central Park. Christo and Jeanne-Claude's artwork was a unique spectacle. Their environmental art inspired millions.

TAKING THEIR TIME

Many works by Christo and Jeanne-Claude took decades from start to finish. The most significant was *Wrapped Reichstag*, a government building in Berlin, Germany. They proposed the idea in 1971. It was finally approved in 1995. Christo and Jeanne-Claude believed this process was part of their artwork.

2

Number of weeks Christo and Jeanne-Claude's artwork have usually lasted.

- Christo and Jeanne-Claude emigrated from France in 1964.
- They became famous for wrapping large structures in cloth.
- Their artwork created unique spectacles and communal events.

Tina Ramirez's Dance Company Speaks a New Language

In 2005, the daughter of a Mexican bullfighter received the highest award given to artists by the US government. The National Medal of Arts honors outstanding artistic contributions to the nation.

Tina Ramirez was born in Venezuela in 1929. Her mother was a Puerto Rican community leader. When her parents divorced in 1936, Ramirez

immigrated to the United States with her mother. She was seven years old.

In New York City, Ramirez began taking dance lessons. She studied Spanish dance from a young age. Her teacher, Lola Bravo, ran a famous dance studio. Ramirez later trained in ballet and modern dance. Growing up, she performed with several dance companies. In the 1950s, she danced in Broadway musicals and on TV.

In 1963, Bravo retired. Ramirez took over her former teacher's dance studio. She turned it into a school. She wanted students to learn about their heritage by studying Spanish dance, music, and language. Students also learned ballet and modern dance. This combination of training was unique at the time. Ramirez also taught parents how to

sew dance costumes. The students often performed in parks, hospitals, and schools.

By the late 1960s, Ramirez's school was busy. But her grown students had no place to perform. Few dance companies were hiring Latino dancers. So Ramirez decided to start a dance company. In 1970, she founded Ballet Hispánico. The company's style was her own blend of ballet, modern, and Spanish dance. Education remained part of her mission. Today Ballet Hispánico performs across the US and around the world.

700
Number of students at Ballet Hispánico School of Dance in 2017.

- Tina Ramirez emigrated from Venezuela when she was seven.
- She was a dancer with training in ballet, modern, and Spanish dance.
- She founded Ballet Hispánico, now a world-famous dance company.

Bette Bao Lord's Stories Reach Across Oceans

When Bette Bao came to the United States, she didn't plan to stay. But US-China relations became a strong force in her life—as a writer and an unofficial diplomat. In 1998, she received the Eleanor Roosevelt Award for Human Rights for her work to improve international relations.

Bette Bao was born in China in 1938. Her father was a Chinese government official. In 1946, because he spoke English, he was sent to work in the United States. Most of the family came along. They meant to stay only a few years. Bette's baby sister, nicknamed Sansan, remained behind with relatives. Bette was eight years old.

In 1949, after a long civil war, the Communists took over the Chinese government. Bette's father had worked for the old Nationalist government. The family could not return home. They were stranded in the United States, and Sansan was still in China.

Bette won a scholarship and went to college. In 1962, Sansan was reunited with her family. Bette

19

Number of languages *Spring Moon* has been published in.

- Bette Bao Lord emigrated from China in 1946.
- She is a writer whose work has helped to improve international relations.
- Her novel *Spring Moon* became a best seller.

was inspired to write her sister's story. She wanted people to know what life in communist China was like for an average person. In 1964, her first book, *Eighth Moon*, was published.

In 1963, Bette married American diplomat Winston Lord. She continued to write. *Spring Moon: A Novel of China* was published in 1982. It became a best seller. Her children's book *In the Year of the Boar and Jackie Robinson*, published in 1984, is now a classic. It tells of her experience as a young immigrant. Bette's books have been published around the world.

Edwidge Danticat's Books Break Through the Silence

Edwidge Danticat grew up in a country where reading was dangerous. She loved books, but in Haiti they were tightly controlled. Owning the wrong book could get you killed.

Danticat was born in Haiti in 1969. At the time, the country was ruled by a dictator. When Danticat was young, her parents immigrated to the United States. They wanted to build a better life for their children. Danticat and her siblings stayed behind and waited. They were raised by their aunt and uncle. In 1981, when Danticat was 12, the family reunited in Brooklyn, New York.

At her new school, Danticat was bullied for being Haitian. As she learned English, she began to write. At age 14, she wrote an article for a youth magazine. It was about her experience immigrating. After it was published, Danticat kept writing. She went to college and graduate school. She worked on a novel based on her experience. In 1994, *Breath, Eyes, Memory* was published. When Oprah Winfrey chose it for her book club in 1998, Danticat became famous.

Danticat's second novel came out the same year. *The Farming of Bones* is about the 1937 massacre of Haitian people living in the Dominican Republic. It won the American Book Award. Danticat's writing often breaks the silence around painful events. In 2009, she was awarded a MacArthur "Genius Grant" for her work.

11
Number of years it took Danticat to write her first novel.

- Edwidge Danticat emigrated from Haiti in 1981.
- She is an award-winning novelist and short-story writer.
- She began her first novel, *Breath, Eyes, Memory,* when she was in high school.

THINK ABOUT IT

Danticat's fictional books are based on real events and experiences. How might a writer's own life influence the stories he or she writes?

Shahzia Sikander's Art Makes the Old New Again

Sikander went to art school. Working with a master teacher, she trained in the ancient art of Indo-Persian miniature painting. Miniatures are small paintings with fine details.

Sikander began using the old techniques to create contemporary art. Her 1992 painting *The Scroll* made traditional miniature painting popular again. The Pakistan embassy in Washington, DC, held a show of her paintings. In 1993, Sikander immigrated to the United States. She went to the Rhode Island School of Design. In 1997, she moved to New York City. Her work was shown at major galleries.

Shahzia Sikander wanted to make art in a different way. She was drawn to an ancient art form that few people cared about. By studying it, she changed how people saw it.

Sikander was born in Pakistan in 1969. Her family encouraged her to draw.

In 2001, Sikander began to animate her miniature paintings. She had taken photos of a painting she was working on. She realized the photos could be turned into animation. In 2015, she created *Gopi Contagion*. It was installed on digital billboards

in Times Square. Animation transformed women's hair into a flock of flying birds.

Sikander was asked to create art for the United States embassy in Pakistan. She received a MacArthur "Genius Grant" in 2006. In 2012, she was awarded the National Medal of Arts.

18

Number of hours Sikander worked every day for four years to master miniature painting.

- Shahzia Sikander emigrated from Pakistan in 1993.
- She is a painter, illustrator, and multimedia artist.
- She is known for reinventing Indo-Persian miniature painting.

PAINTING IN MINIATURE

People learn Indo-Persian miniature painting by becoming apprentices. They work under master teachers. They practice by copying paintings made by the masters. First they trace outlines with black ink. Then they apply thin layers of watercolor. Small details are painted with squirrel hair brushes.

Michel Kouakou's Dance Connects Four Continents

coins. He used the money to pay for school. When he grew older, he joined a dance crew. The group danced in local street competitions.

When Kouakou was 15, a dance teacher saw him perform. She brought him to her school for training. Kouakou studied acrobatics and contemporary dance. When he was 18, civil war broke out in Ivory Coast. He fled to Belgium to continue his training. Kouakou studied dance in Europe and Asia. In 2003, he began to teach and choreograph. He started a dance company called Daara Dance. Kouakou immigrated to the Unites States in 2004.

Michel Kouakou believes that art is everywhere, and dance can come from anywhere. By his mid-20s, he had traveled and trained in many countries. His global perspective on art comes from his own experiences.

Kouakou was born in 1981 in Côte d'Ivoire (Ivory Coast), Africa. His family was large and had little money. As a child, Kouakou began dancing for spare

In New York City, Kouakou developed his choreography skills. His dance style was inspired by all the places he had trained. He combined tribal dance from Ivory Coast, Japanese Butoh dance, and contemporary dance. Kouakou became known as

a brilliant, risk-taking choreographer. His work gathers together many traditions and reworks them into something new. He translates between different languages of dance movement. Daara Dance now performs worldwide.

Kouakou has taught dance across the United States and around the world. In 2012, he was awarded two important prizes for his creative work. In 2016, he joined the dance faculty at the University of Minnesota. He continues building artistic bridges between cultures.

10
Number of countries Kouakou's dance company has performed in, as of 2017.

- Michel Kouakou emigrated from Ivory Coast to escape war.
- He is an award-winning dancer and choreographer.
- His innovative choreography combines tribal and contemporary dance.

Thomas Nast

The first great American cartoonist was born in Germany in 1840. Thomas Nast immigrated to the United States in 1846. As a political cartoonist, he targeted corrupt politicians. He popularized the donkey and elephant as symbols of the Democratic and Republican political parties.

The "Long" and "Short" of it is a general "Bust" up in the "Street."

Frances Hodgson Burnett

An English immigrant wrote the classic books *The Secret Garden* and *A Little Princess*. Frances Hodgson Burnett was born in 1849. In 1865, she came to the United States with her penniless family. She began writing to make money. Burnett became a celebrated novelist and short story writer.

Xavier Martínez

San Francisco's arts scene owes much to Xavier Martínez. Born in 1869, Martínez was a painter who hosted weekly open houses. He arrived in the city in 1893, having left Mexico to attend art school. Martínez helped develop California's Tonalist painting style and its arts community.

Edward Steichen

Edward Steichen's fashion photography defined *Vogue* and *Vanity Fair* during the 1920s. Born in Luxembourg in 1879, Steichen immigrated as a child in 1881. During the 1910s, he developed his precise artistic style in France. His work became the template for American fashion photography.

Editor's note:
America is a nation of immigrants. This series celebrates important contributions immigrants have made to the arts. In choosing the people to feature in this book, the author and 12-Story Library editors considered diversity of all kinds and the significance and stature of the work. This book focuses on visual arts, literature, and dance. Another volume in this series, *12 Immigrants Who Made American Entertainment Great,* focuses on music, theater, and film.

Glossary

art movement
A style of art created by a group of artists during a specific time period.

choreography
The sequence of movements in a dance. Also, the art of designing that sequence.

communal
Shared by a community or other group of people.

contemporary art
Art created in the late 1900s through the early 2000s.

improvisation
The art of creating or performing without preparation, using only what is available at the moment.

innovative
New, original, or creative.

massacre
A mass killing of a group of people.

modern art
Art created in the late 1800s to the late 1900s.

multimedia art
Art that uses more than one form of media. For example, sculpture (visual) with sound (audio).

symbol
A sign or shape that represents a more complex idea.

translate
To change words or ideas from one language into another language.

undocumented
Lacking a document that proves legal residency.

For More Information

Books

Furgang, Adam. *Famous Immigrant Artists*. New York: Enslow, 2018.

Greenberg, Jan, and Sandra Jordan. *Christo and Jeanne-Claude: Through the Gates and Beyond*. New York: Roaring Brook Press, 2008.

Rohmer, Harriet, ed. *Just Like Me: Stories and Self-Portraits by Fourteen Artists*. San Francisco, CA: Children's Book Press, 2013.

Visit 12StoryLibrary.com

Scan the code or use your school's login at **12StoryLibrary.com** for recent updates about this topic and a full digital version of this book. Enjoy free access to:

- Digital ebook
- Breaking news updates
- Live content feeds
- Videos, interactive maps, and graphics
- Additional web resources

Note to educators: Visit 12StoryLibrary.com/register to sign up for free premium website access. Enjoy live content plus a full digital version of every 12-Story Library book you own for every student at your school.

Index

About the Author

Tristan Poehlmann is a freelance writer of educational nonfiction. He holds a master's degree in writing for children and young adults from Vermont College of Fine Arts. He lives in the San Francisco Bay Area.